You can do better than that!

Second Chances...

YVONNE HAMPDEN

COPYRIGHT © 2018, Yvonne Hampden

ISBN: 978-0-9744086-3-7

All rights reserved. No part of this book may be reproduced or transmitted in any form or by any means, electronic or mechanical, including photocopying, recording or by any information storage and retrieval system, without permission in writing from the publisher or author.

For information address:

A YMAH RIVERA PUBLICATION
yhampden@yahoo.com

Edited by Yvonne Hampden

Layout, Design: Jonathan Gullery.

FIRST EDITION

Inspired by my lover
MIGUEL

My dad fell from grace and experienced spiritual death, what we often call depression, after his mother died. He was dysfunctional. Many years later, he admitted he was a gigolo and had hurt mom.

Mom talked with me about this, near our living room window, many years ago. We were home alone that day, cleaning the house, washing clothes and putting them away in drawers.

I accidentally knocked her orange porcelain vase over.

It hit the ground and broke.

Nevertheless, she was kind to me, but nothing was the same in her life after that day.

HI

A time before mom was laid to rest she revealed to me her feelings about people, "Everybody's sick," she said. I knew that meant she was sick too.

I guess she understood then that I was still able to love.

No matter what, I still believed in my

ability to love, and be loved in return.

Lessons were taught, as I continued to develop my courage, and faith; I had learned to trust and follow my heart.

I gave myself the time and dedication it takes to listen to my heart… and figure things out with wisdom. We all have the same qualities.

I still sit in the silence waiting for love to reveal itself to me; always searching my heart for my heart's answers.

Here are lessons I've learned to survive these changing times.

I am revealing them to you because all of us can do better.

So, please, take your brokenness and by the Hand of God may we all be made whole again.

I'm grateful for my broken heart… I found real love because of it, was given a second chance. You owe it to yourself to find out. How would we even know the difference, if we didn't have something to compare it with?

Well, my dad lived most of his young life

dysfunctional, and mom searched for the love she couldn't replace that she had for dad.

…What goes around comes around….

There's his story, there's her story… Then there's the Truth.

We've heard it all before …Forgiveness… It's the key!

WHAT LOVE HAS REVEALED TO ME/PROGRESS...

Just for Today

Chances Are...

Women will marry powerful men
to have them help survive their families.

Just for Today

Chances Are…

Guilt, fear and anger can overwhelm you in this life, especially when you are hurt. So, to avoid falling apart you must know the difference between what is real & what is unreal.

Just for Today

※※※※※

Chances Are...

If you are dealing with guilt or shame you may no longer want to accept those feelings about what someone else did, or how they felt about you.

Feelings seem to control a large part of our reality.

Just for Today

Chances Are…

Spiritual Warfare is real, so give rise to it.

Don't be afraid… be true to your Heart.

Only love is real, believe in yourself.

Protect yourself, and don't trust anyone else

to find solutions for you.

Take refuge in the Lord.

Just for Today

Chances Are...

Practice forgiveness: It keeps our hearts true.

Just for Today

Chances Are...

Children are the victims of their parent's circumstances. It may be wise to give yourself the time & dedication needed to figure things out, once you are out of your parents' home.

Just for Today

Chances Are...

Our Souls belong to God - Our One True Love...

By the Hand of God all good remains.

Just for Today

Chances Are...

When we surrender our Will over to God

he ensures our safe keeping... We are saved.

Just for Today

Chances Are...

Life is a gamble, love as well.

Never show anyone your whole hand...

but, you better play your cards right.

Think about this:

The Upper Hand will not

outweigh a True Heart.

Just for Today

Chances Are...

People will follow their natural resources in order to survive. This may be why there is so much migration in the world.

Just for Today

Chances Are...

Take a leap of faith.

They are not risk but a desire

for something more.

When temptation comes refuse to be vain...

She only wants to know if you're true.

Just for Today

Chances Are...

Take the time to search your heart,

listen to your heart... follow the truth

of what your heart is saying:

Nothing's free and it takes two to dance:

you will either be partners and best friends,

or worst enemies.

Remember: you are in it

together... Do the work.

You may get a Second Chance.

Just for Today

Chances Are...
While being a good provider and
relying on yourself is important,
you may create a false sense of security
with others because you may become unhappy
if your needs are not met.

Just for Today

Chances Are...

A person who pays the cost to be the boss
will want to have his cake and eat it too.

Just for Today

Chances Are...

Be happy with yourself,

then your joy will be complete.

Don't compete with others,

everyone has their own vision.

Just for Today

Chances Are...

Avoid contemplating what others think about you if you're not willing to change.

Just for Today

Chances Are...

Getting too complacent may be an issue...

the rug can be pulled from

under you at any time.

Just for Today

Chances Are...
Remember to forgive yourself for the mistakes
you've made in your lifetime...
it can make the difference between
sickness and health... even Death.

Just for Today

Chances Are...

We all deserve to be loved, if you would only believe you are worthy of it. You never know whose heart you've touched & healed, until they've touched and healed yours.

Just for Today

Chances Are...

Life is a Mirror, Love is a Cure All,

Truth is a Cleanser, and Spirit Speaks to us All.

It will take a village to grow evenly.

Just for Today

Chances Are...
Crimes of the heart may be forgiven,
remember to be accountable for your behavior.

Just for Today

Chances Are...

Exodus 34:14

God is a jealous God... put no one before him.

Honorable Men have the attributes of God.

Always respect yourself in that regard.

Just for Today

Chances Are...

Don't look back... You will only

hit up against a wall.

Your heart may turn to stone.

Just for Today

Chances Are...

The choice to live or die is a very personal choice...

Do whatever makes you the happiest.

Just for Today

Chances Are...

If you like your Spouse, and he likes you...

your bond of love won't be broken.

Just for Today

Chances Are...

Your Wedding Ring is between your legs,

and the finger it is placed on is your Man's penis.

Practice Chasity.

That's the way Nature planned it.

Just for Today

Chances Are...

Always Pray for each other,

if one of us is happy and the other unhappy.

Show you care... Miracles can happen.

Just for Today

Chances Are...

It's nice to have tangible things that

reflect the love in our lives...

but, one's true possession is of the heart. ...

and, the presence of a loved one is

more valuable than anything money can buy.

Just for Today

Chances Are...

When we Step-up and take on our responsibilities as an adult and protect our children...Lives are not only saved, children will learn to value themselves and will not allow abuse in their lives.

Just for Today

>>>>≪≪≪

Chances Are...

Our skin may be the largest organ of our body.

Intact skin is our body's first line of

defense against infection.

Remember this when you

consider body art/tattoo's.

Just for Today

Chances Are...

Abortion, Prison Confinement,

the premeditated killing of people of Color and

Homosexuality is all connected to DNA & Gene survival.

These human life issues must be dealt with.

Just for Today

Chances Are…

Your Power is within you; do not surrender it to anyone.

Stand in your Truth.

Just for Today

Chances Are...

Our Service to others and our giving to others

in the World is the Rent we pay to God

for our life here on Earth.

Just for Today

Chances Are...

When we break a person's spirit &
teach them to conform to our image of them
we can mold them into anything
we want them to be: A criminal, a soldier,
a slave, a Leader... a person of good Will,
and good deeds...
a good citizen, even a Priest.

Just for Today

Chances Are...

Love can sometimes weaken the spirit.
We try so hard to show we care. Then we try
to take care of the person who is hurting.
If we let go & let God it may make
the difference between someone learning
to love themselves. Giving them
enough time to figure things out and
find what they've learned
from their experience.

Just for Today

Chances Are...

We are all learning from each other.

The information you have and identify with,

plus intuition from all sources of life:

School, Church, Community-People,

Places and Things will be like

Deja vu - Suck it up.

You are getting closer to the Goal.

Just for Today

Chances Are...

Take nothing for granted,
listen & look for signs... They are the
landmarks for love.
Then let life, love, truth and spirit
work itself out. Claim your good...
Confirm your good by giving thanks
to your Higher Power.
Seal it with a Kiss!

Just for Today

Chances Are...

Burning desires are our Hearts fire.

There is a Divine Revelation...

Truth is being revealed...

Once again, stand in your Truth!

Claim your Good!

Just for Today

꠶꠶꠶꠶꠶꠶

Chances Are...

Young people may be naïve

losing their innocence at a young age.

But, don't give yourself away...

Don't give away your Gem.

Know within yourself where

the other person ends and where you begin.

It's wise to be old-fashioned and have a chaperone

when you date. Many women end up with unwanted

pregnancies that could have been prevented.

Just for Today

Chances Are...

Adolescence is a time when we explore our sexual feelings. When we violate each other, or go too far and are not responsible we end up becoming adult children. Adult children who are traumatized by these events may experience a broken heart. It is mandatory that you keep your boundaries. Get the emotional support you need.

Just for Today

Chances Are...

Addiction may begin with Chocolate, Caffeine teas & coffee, Colas, Cigarettes & Cigars, Energy Drinks (Red Bull, etc.), Liquor, Marijuana, Hash, Cocaine and/or Opioids. Some psychiatric medicines and medications like Neurontin may affect the CNS, too. The CNS is our Central Nervous System - Our Brain (Power Center), and our Spinal Cord. We block feelings of pleasure, while we do our best to block feelings of pain.

Just for Today

Chances Are...

Earth was once a Paradise full of rich soil, Sun and rain. The waters were clean & the Air was unpolluted. Can Fire change the World? We are still learning how. So, eat your fruits & vegetables and enjoy the Earth. Mother Nature has given us everything. Remember, everything that is in the Soil is in our Food & Water.

Just for Today

Chances Are...
We work so hard for things not worth having that distracts us from our natural cycle of life.

Just for Today

Chances Are...

Doctors, Lawyers, Clergy, Teachers, Politicians,

and First Responders-Do they really care?

When people in these positions really care,

Miracles happen in our lives,

especially at the Grass Root level.

There is a positive chain reaction...

But the Meek shall inherit the earth;

Psalms 37:11.

Just for Today

Chances Are...

Human trafficking-Slavery in our modern day society-

Is less about production & economy,

and more about the World Governments

allowing the Institution of Prostitution

legal in some parts of the World.

Children are our easiest prey. Why is

the rape of Innocence so widely accepted?

Why is it so necessary to eat our young?

Just for Today

Chances Are…

Our Children may be receiving

too many cancer causing - free radicals into their

underdeveloped bodies - does it matter where the free

radicals come from? Protect yourself and your children.

Breastfeeding is Mother Nature's

way of protecting our children

from anything harmful

in the environment.

Just for Today

≫≪

Chances Are...

The Public School System in the USA is designed to

house our children while parents work & earn money to

support their family's lifestyle, pay bills

and the cost of health insurance.

Homeschool your children if you can,

their lives may be saved from the violent attacks

on the USA Public School System.

Just for Today

Chances Are...

Our future... here on planet Earth

...Belongs to those who invest in it.

Just for Today

Chances Are...

When you become a victim of circumstances

It's nobody's fault...

You can either fall from Grace...

Or, simply fight to survive the war.

Pick & choose your battles,

surrender your Will over to God.

Just for Today

Chances Are...

Like the Wizard of OZ...

It takes Courage ...Don't give up.

You will need your Heart

...Searching to find who you belong to.

Please, by all means use your Brain

...Give yourself the time and dedication

you will need to figure things out.

Remember, you can go Home at any time.

Just for Today

༺༻

Chances Are…

Mostly, every one of us has Jesus' Soul.

We sacrifice & give of ourselves selflessly

without complaining or even explaining

our own personal circumstances.

We commit to loving each other & like our

Moms did take care of and nurse

each other back to health…

Even helping others escape Death,

or persecution.

Just for Today

Chances Are...

Then, you will be renewed by God

with what I like to call being

a witness to his Miracles.

Just for Today

Chances Are...

When your Man ages & his belly

extends before he's old

will he still be attractive to you?

Just think... He is so full of your love it may

look like he's pregnant... He just may be.

He may be giving birth to the second part of his life,

because you have given him a second chance.

Remember, it's a choice!

Just for Today

Chances Are…

The Struggle… is personal, within ourselves…

"Will I take that Leap of Faith,

is it too much of a Risk?"

Just for Today

Chances Are...
A Soldier coming out of battle has suffered
a Spiritual death. He will only be
redeemed by the Will of God.

Just for Today

※※※

Chances Are...

It's all good... There is no right or wrong,

only a need to fulfill it!

It is not for us to fulfill it,

but God, Our One True Love!

Just for Today

Chances Are...

Rely on yourself because you can.

You have your own abilities as a Child of God.

You are able until you are unable.

Just for Today

Chances Are...

Everyone's got something in their lifetime,

such as a disability, an addiction, a broken heart,

a loss of someone or something...

poverty, ignorance or an inability to learn.

So, hold on to your gifts & talents...

tangible or intangible... they are the difference between

the challenges and Miracles in your life.

Just for Today

※※※※

Chances Are...

Mostly, everyone has a Good side

& a bad side... a strong side & a weak side...

a healthy side & an unhealthy side.

We depend on and practice

Homeostasis = Balance.

Just for Today

Chances Are...

The idea is to function in your life...
but, if you want to be happy
you got to do the work.
School, Church, therapy, self-help books,
and a good listener like a friend or Minister
may allow you some form of inspiration.

Just for Today

Chances Are...
To 'listen' means being still & silent
and hearing the meaning
of your speaker with your heart and mind,
what someone is conveying to you.

Just for Today

Chances Are...

While living with an open-mind

keep your wants and desires simple.

Just for Today

Chances Are...

If you choose to believe in love...

and, Second Chances remember...

'It's in the Bag.'

Godspeed!

About Second Chances

Many adolescent experiences in the United States & around the World are met with emotional neglect, sexual violations, physical abuse, Homelessness and unwanted pregnancies with broken family ties. Adolescents may become drug or alcohol dependent and make use of any time in prison confinement.

As individuals, we often move on with our day-to-day living, and may meet people or read books about people with interesting lives and stories to share.

When inspired by others we sometimes feel we see our reflection in a mirror. When I began my search within for my salvation I remarried an honorable military veteran. Together, we created a love affair that included communicating our needs.

We overachieved in our work ethics, and we returned to school: I became a Nurse, and ten years later earned my degree in Liberal Arts in Humanities. While my husband trained as a CDL Commercial Truck Driver, after retiring from

NYC Housing as a Maintenance and Oil Burner Technician.

You can achieve your goals too; keep up the good work...

>   *When you get too tired, Rest...*
>   *When you get too hungry, Eat...*
>   *When you get too angry, Make amends...*
>   *When you get too broke, create a nest egg.*

Yvonne Hampden has been happily married for more than 30 years.

www.ingramcontent.com/pod-product-compliance
Lightning Source LLC
Chambersburg PA
CBHW050558300426
44112CB00013B/1968